TOP TIPS:
ALL-AGE WORSHIP

Nick Harding

Copyright © 2005
First published 2005
Reprinted 2007
ISBN 978 1 84427 125 2

Scripture Union, 207–209 Queensway,
Bletchley, Milton Keynes, MK2 2EB,
England
Email: info@scriptureunion.org.uk
Website: www.scriptureunion.org.uk

Scripture Union Australia
Locked Bag 2, Central Coast Business
Centre, NSW 2252
Website: www.scriptureunion.org.au

Scripture Union USA
PO Box 987,Valley Forge, PA 19482
Website: www.scriptureunion.org

The right of Nick Harding to be
identified as author of this work has
been asserted by him in accordance
with the Copyright, Designs and
Patents Act 1988

British Library Cataloguing-in-
Publication Data.
A catalogue record of this book is
available from the British Library.

Printed and bound in Dorchester,
England by Henry Ling.

Logo and cover design:
www.splash-design.co.uk

Internal design:
www.splash-design.co.uk

Internal illustrations:
Colin Smithson

Scripture Union is an
international Christian charity working
with churches in more than 130
countries, providing resources to bring
the good news about Jesus Christ to
children, young people and families
and to encourage them to develop
spiritually through the Bible and
prayer.

As well as our network of volunteers,
staff and associates who run holidays,
church-based events and school
Christian groups, we produce a wide
range of publications and support
those who use our resources through
training programmes.

INTRODUCTION

One of the challenges facing churches today is to find the best ways to plan, develop and lead worship for all ages.

All-age worship :
- welcomes all ages in the church family
- helps young and old alike spend time together
- is appropriate for everyone there
- enables people of all ages to worship God and meet with him.

If we take church attendance figures too seriously, the dramatic fall in the numbers of children and teenagers in the church would cause despair. But I see signs of hope in the excitement, fun and profound spiritual development that takes place during what we used to call 'family services'. All-age worship is for many churches a growth area, reaching out to children, young people and families through events, mission and evangelism and providing worship that is welcoming and nurturing.

Is your church ready?
Looking at all-age worship, we'll recognise the key reasons why it is such a vital area. It isn't only about meeting the needs of the whole congregation, regardless of age or background. It is also about helping all ages to worship our great God with wonder. A community of faith should be a community who worship and learn as one, not in fractured groups. This book offers lots of basic ideas but to make all-age worship really work you need to graft in your own vision, gifts and ideas.

THE ALL-AGE CHURCH AND ALL-AGE WORSHIP

Most churches would say that they cater for all ages. Yet in reality much about our churches, from the furniture and facilities to the relevance and relationships, is organised by and designed for adults. The best all-age worship comes when it is rooted in a true all-age church. It may require a fundamental change in the mind-set and management lines of the church. This may seem impossible but don't panic. The aim of this book is to suggest how your church could move forward. But first of all, what is all-age worship?

An all-age church is...

....Open to all ages
Everybody in the community of the church – children, teenagers, parents, single adults or older members – is welcomed and encouraged. No one feels excluded, undervalued or unable to make a contribution. All worshippers learn to accept and value each other.

Older members learn to welcome the contribution of young children and families, along with any disruption that accompanies this. Those who prefer exuberant worship learn to appreciate quieter, reflective styles of worship.

....Shaped by all ages
The structures are such that everybody is represented when decisions are made about how the church grows and develops. Just as there is a forum for the adults, there is also a forum for children and teenagers to contribute to key decisions that affect them.

The consequences for worship will be that all ages participate fully and have roles in the planning, delivery and leadership.

....Investing in all-ages

Many church budgets are set in favour of adult worship, music, equipment, comforts and facilities. An all-age church will consciously and openly invest in children and teenagers by providing good facilities, leaders, training and resources.

Worship will represent the spending priorities of the church, with equipment, facilities and delivery of the highest standard.

In reality...

A small village Baptist church following the example of the village school, provided young people with a forum to make suggestions and see changes. In school they call it 'School Council', in the church it is 'Children's Committee'. Six children represent the age range and discuss the worship, their own group activities and even what they think of the minister! This is not tokenism – their suggestions do make a difference.

....Counter-cultural

Unlike many situations in our society today, there are no barriers between old and young and no mistrust across the generations. The church is not a ghetto where only certain people or groups are allowed. In-jokes that exclude, and unkind 'put-downs' are not heard.

Worship operates with a genuinely integrated approach in mind, encouraging people of all ages to build relationships so that they pray, teach and learn from each other. Children and young people are involved in prayer and ministry, praying for and with adults as well as peers.

Think about...

What can be done in your church to help people of different ages interact and work better together? Could older people pray for and mentor younger ones? (There must be suitable facilities and child protection measures in place.)

Could young people help older ones in spiritual and practical ways?

....Serving the community

The needs, levels of understanding and cultural backgrounds of those in the community outside church will be central to the planning. An all-age church will seek to draw people from the community into the church community.

Worship takes the needs of visitors into account. Visitors are courteously asked about their religious background, experience and expectations.

....Committed to moving forward

The all-age church does not stand still. This is the 21st century! Meaningful and relevant approaches to worship, service and teaching are encouraged.

This all-age church makes full use of technology to communicate in relevant ways to people of all backgrounds. The ways children and young people learn is always recognised.

Have a look at: *Learning Styles*, Marlene le Fever (Kingsway)
Kids Culture, Nick Harding (Scripture Union)
Children Finding Faith, Francis Bridger (Scripture Union)
Creating a Learning Church, Margaret Cooling (BRF)

....Serving all-ages

Activities, events and teaching at the level required by different ages

and understanding, will be
provided. There will be times for
new Christians to learn
together, for older people to
gather for fellowship and for
younger people to be taught.
Home groups and cell groups
for a mix of ages and
backgrounds are found.

There must also be times
when the whole church comes
together as a family to worship.
At this point, toddlers may be given
'useful bags' containing quiet, interesting items. A service when
all are together is a key time for all to share and learn. It should never
lead to adults saying, 'That was nice for the kiddies' at the end of a
service.

Think about...

- How do people in your congregation
help others to find their way through the
worship?
- Are there people who will welcome or
sit with visitors to help them?
- Are all-age services led in a way that
helps those who are not regular
attenders?

####....Valuing everyone, whatever their role
Everybody respects those, (usually about 20%), who do most of the
work to keep the church moving forward. This church encourages
children and young people to value their leaders, and adults to take
delight in the gifts of the youngsters. The services provide an
opportunity to thank all those who serve God in the church,
appreciate the gifts of others, and pray for those with
leadership responsibilities.

####....The responsibility of all
All ages will be encouraged to pray for the church,
contribute their skills and give both time and money.

All-age worship will be attended by a good cross-section of the church community. Parents will want to encourage their children to worship here and older members will relish the opportunity to be with younger worshippers.

....Full of variety

An all-age church will relish different traditions and bring the best of worship, prayer and music from many styles, celebrating difference while striving for unity. All-age worship lends itself to variety. This enables everyone to participate and receive something special.

....Committed to ministry, growing gifts and abilities

An all-age church will be actively looking out for those with gifts, abilities and potential for ministry. When the church sees people with gifts, whatever their age, it will offer training and mentoring and will provide opportunities to minister within the body of the church. Expectations will be realistic and comments helpful. It will be OK to make (and learn from) mistakes.

....A place of tolerance

We do not choose our own family! Likewise, God has placed us in a local church family. We may have personality clashes with others and we may speak up against things we don't like but, as we strive for unity, we may have to put our differences aside for the sake of the church community.

Not every aspect of an all-age service will appeal to all people all of the time. It is like an evening's TV viewing – something for most people, but never everything for everyone. It is very sad if people decide that the all-age worship morning is the Sunday when they can vote with their feet.

....Upside-down

Echoing the upside-down values of the kingdom of God, all-age church is where those with the least access to power and authority are consciously supported and encouraged to make a difference. The pyramid of church leader, elders or PCC at the top with children, young people, older people and new members at the bottom is inverted.

Worship in the upside-down all-age church will be radical, exciting, risky and full of challenge! How does your church shape up against these ideals of the all-age church? Set out an action plan to move things forward and don't give up.

In your action plan consider:
- Training and encouraging leaders
- A realistic timescale to integrate all ages
- Revision of the decision-making structures
- Consultation within the church and community
- Education and encouragement of the congregation

Think about...

What would be the reaction of your church congregation if any of the following arrived unexpectedly?
- A group of teenagers from the local estate
- A group of adults with learning difficulties
- A single mother with three under 5's
- Six older people from the local nursing home

2   PRACTICAL ALL-AGE WORSHIP

There are many practical components for effective all-age worship. It takes time to prepare them, to put them together in the right order and make them work well. Most of the congregation will not realise the care and skill that has been invested into making it run properly, but they'll know if it doesn't work!

Timing

- Some churches are restricted to when they can hold all-age events and services. This may be due to pressures felt by leaders involved in leading worship in more than one church, or the fact that a church building accommodates a number of congregations. Services too early on a Sunday morning may not attract families with children aged over five, or large families. The weekday pressures of getting everyone up and ready do not need to be repeated on a Sunday!
- Services too late on a Sunday morning may not attract families that are busy visiting relatives or spending the day on leisure activities. There is not enough time left to make the most of the day.
- For the thousands of children and young people who spend Sundays or weekends with their non-resident parent, Sunday worship simply does not work.
- Evening worship may work, allowing people to have a day of leisure and rounding it off with fellowship. Evenings in the winter are not popular with older people but good for teenagers (who will be out of bed by then!)
- Midweek all-age worship can work, especially if held in the right place. No late afternoon or early evening slot will suit everyone, but many will see it as a time when they can relax a little more.
- The length of an all-age service should reflect the make-up of the congregation in terms of age profile, background, familiarity with

worship and ability to concentrate. A good target is 45 minutes and leaves people wanting a little more and relishing the extra few minutes to catch up on each other's news over refreshments.

Location

Many churches have to use the main church building for worship. Yet some church buildings are inflexible, difficult to use creatively, and full of sound and sight-line problems. There is something special about meeting for worship in church, but there is also something special about losing some of the 'churchianity' trappings and being creative in a more flexible space.

• All-age worship works well in a church hall, community centre or school venue. This is a particularly valuable option when the church itself is located away from the centre of population.

• All-age worship can use the visual and physical stimuli of a traditional church building to enhance worship.

• All-age worship on a different day of the week and in a different place, perhaps after the school day in a local school, will attract a new group of people and families.

• Church buildings can be associated with funerals, darkness and misery, frightening places for anyone, adult or child, who is not used to them. A neutral venue overcomes this. The occasional change of venue back to the church building may then encourage people unfamiliar with church to cross the threshold.

• How comfortable is your church? Are there toilets and nappy-

In reality…

One minister is delighted to be able to hold all-age services in a local community centre. She says, 'It is the only place in the area where most people go at some time or another. The adults as well as children are not scared to go through the door. It's a different matter at my church!'

changing facilities? Is there running water? Physical discomfort does not usually encourage people to find spiritual comfort! If the church building discourages people from attending because it is an unwelcoming environment then look for another venue.

- Children and young people may perceive the church building as a place for adults and therefore adult territory. To encourage all ages to see it as their space, think about new notice boards, photos, displays, child-friendly furniture and space for young people to congregate.

Sight and Sound

Technical issues need technically-minded people to work with them. For the congregation to get the most out of all-age worship it is essential that everything can be seen and heard.
- Sight lines should be checked from all areas of the church. Very often, pillars or furniture block areas at the front of church, so think carefully where you place visual aids and screens, and how mobile the leaders need to be in order to engage with everyone. Small children will struggle to see over the rows of chairs or pews, but inviting the children to the front for the whole of the service negates some of the principles of the all-age church.
- Visual images and words should be large and attractive. Overhead projector words should be large, (maximum 6 lines per

sheet), and always printed in a clear font and in bold. With current technological development in data projection, many churches are being much more creative in the projection of words for songs and prayers, and images to enhance reflection and worship. However, all projection systems should be able to work in clear sunlight unless the venue has blackouts. They should be checked and ready before the service. It is wise to have spare bulbs in stock, although data projector bulbs often cost up to £400! Remember to keep electric cables in safe positions.

> **Think about...**
>
> • Ask the church leadership whether any thought has ever been given to the timing and venue of all-age services.
>
> • Conduct a survey amongst the church congregation about when they would like services.
>
> • Seek ways to get information and preferences from the wider community.

• Visual image technology such as Powerpoint projection or overhead projectors can be used to display the notices or a message of welcome as people arrive.
• Visual aids like cards, costumes, interesting containers, display boards and puppets should be large enough and high enough for everyone to see.
• Church sound systems vary enormously and not all churches have any form of amplification. A balance has to be struck between the setting up of microphones dominating the service preparation, and the frequent and embarrassing 'Is this on yet?' scenario. As all-age services are likely to involve a number of voices and activity, the sound system needs to be able to cope and those leading worship need to know how to use the equipment for optimum results. If there is a sound system, use it, as many have loop induction systems for those with hearing aids.

- Those with a speaking role in a service should be shown how to speak into a microphone and be trained in speaking to a church congregation. Key points to remember are:

  Keep it slow. Nervous speakers and readers will naturally speed up, so they need to be very aware of how fast they are going.

  Speak clearly. Unless you are a 'roaming reporter' start speaking only when you are in position. Churches have dead spots for sound and often areas where sound echoes. Clear words delivered with a level volume and tone will reach most people.

  Speak confidently. Make sure you have full attention. Difficult Biblical names and places should always be spoken with bravado as no one will know whether they have been pronounced properly! A speaker who struggles will get a wave of sympathy from the congregation, but that will detract from understanding.

- If there are times when people from the congregation speak out loud, either take them to a microphone or repeat in full what they have said. If those who speak are facing the front, anyone behind will not catch much of what they say.

Planning and Leadership

The key to creativity is to work with other people and make the most of the creative synergy that results! Planning good all-age worship needs time, effort and vision.

- Members of a planning group should think through the theme and/or Bible passage before meeting so that they come with ideas. Pray together, establish the objective of the worship session and discuss the theme. The planning group does not necessarily have to include those who lead the service, but if it doesn't, it is more difficult to ensure that the aims of the group are passed on to those who will be delivering it.

• Limit the number and length of notices. Most notices will only be relevant to a few people and almost certainly not for the visitors or young people. Put them on the screen at the start of the service. See the notices from the congregation's point of view.

• Encourage those who are developing their gifts to take part in leading all-age worship. Give them a small activity to lead or a prayer to say at first, and then develop their role. Let it be seen that gender and background do not prevent involvement. Remember that the multi-gifted (such as church leaders) may not be gifted in leading all-age worship.

• Make sure that anyone doing anything in the service is fully briefed with the service order.

• Pray before the service and talk through all of the component parts. Check that all the props and visual aids are in place and that all taking part have arrived.

• Begin the service on time, even if the majority of the congregation have got into the habit of arriving late.

• Try to lead the service with confidence and clarity. Here are a few pointers:

Link the items with a word or two about how they fit the theme, making reference to page or paragraph numbers if appropriate.

Direct by including phrases like 'Let's stand together' and 'We say together' for those who don't know our secret language!

Flow through by avoiding embarrassing gaps when other people come out to do their 'bit' or while microphones are exchanged, but always be careful that unscheduled 'asides' are appropriate.

Unruffled leadership means that if things do not go to plan, as may happen, then everything keeps moving and the attention of the worshippers is kept on what God is saying rather than on the mistakes. **Respond** to the body language and other unspoken messages that the congregation give. Signs of lethargy require something active. A puzzled look requires an explanation. If there are yawns, sing a really loud song, open a window and have a stretch! Some days worship leading is like stirring set concrete, but other days you'll struggle to keep hold of the worshippers. That's just the way it is.

• Those who are willing to serve God in upfront roles are often very vulnerable straight after taking part in a service, so don't wade in instantly with criticisms and complaints. However, feedback is important at some point afterwards.

• Consult the congregation from time to time about what they enjoy and dislike. The congregation can spot issues about sound, vision, delivery and effectiveness. Take on board suggestions, but remember, it is impossible to please everyone.

Creative Components

All-age worship will be a challenge for some and a joy for others. If it is to be successful, it needs to be creative and to challenge the traditional ways that worship takes place.

• If there are creative activities planned, consider how much legitimate havoc they will cause. Be careful about the use of paint and glue in order to avoid damage to carpets, furniture and clothes.

• Prayer activities are often practical and physical, but usually need space. Plan activities that are suitable for the room you have. Remember that fixed chairs and pews present barriers.

• Try to be realistic about the time it takes to do creative things with a large group of people. The more people there are, the longer it takes to give things out, turn into groups, join hands or respond to questions. If

there is formal feedback from discussion groups, this will eat up time.
- Think through the order of the service so that there is a good balance with plenty of time for quiet and reflection and activity. With our hectic lifestyles it is perhaps more important than ever that harassed parents, worried grandparents and ultra-busy young people have space to think and find a little peace.
- If there are other exceptional components to the all-age worship such as a Thanksgiving, Dedication or Baptism, or the commissioning of workers or missionaries, make sure that adequate time is given. Also remember a large group of visitors will change the atmosphere of the worship. Active and creative elements may be more difficult to deliver.

> **Think about...**
>
> Many people would play a part if they were asked to... personally! Appeals for help don't usually work. Identify appropriate people and ask them directly. Is there anyone you could draw into an all-age planning team or who may have worship leadership gifts lying dormant? Are there children or teenagers who are obviously talented but who would not want to push themselves forward?

- Will the visual aids, dramatic games and active prayers live on in the memory longer than the theme or message?
- 'Keep it short, keep it simple.' Enough said for now? I think so!

3 INNOVATIVE ALL-AGE WORSHIP

What are the key components in worship? If that question were easy to answer then the Christian church would be much more united and worship would be much less varied in different places!

The key components in your church may be some of the things on this list, but probably not all of them. Tick those that are regular parts of your all-age worship and then check out those that you do not do. Could you be more varied and creative, benefiting from other traditions?

- [ ] Set order of service
- [ ] Worship songs for older people
- [ ] Worship songs for younger people
- [ ] Confession
- [ ] Offering
- [ ] Opportunity for interaction
- [ ] Item for very young children
- [ ] All-age Communion
- [ ] Physical prayer
- [ ] Time for ministry and prayer
- [ ] Bible reading
- [ ] Story
- [ ] Something to take away

- [ ] Traditional hymns
- [ ] Worship songs for all ages
- [ ] Liturgy
- [ ] Quiet
- [ ] Discussion
- [ ] Game or quiz
- [ ] Making or doing activity
- [ ] Intercessory prayer
- [ ] People praying for each other
- [ ] Formal beginning and ending
- [ ] Talk
- [ ] Application for all ages

Putting the components together

The list above highlights both the various possibilities and the exciting challenges of getting a balance when assembling the component parts of an all-age worship service.

- Worship needs to include an element of tradition and ritual in order for those present to feel comfortable enough to relax. We all need boundaries and even the most reluctant teenagers will gain from knowing that there is some form of structure to the worship.

- Worship needs to have a clear beginning and a definite ending along with guidance throughout, so that all know what they should and should not be doing. Be clear about the space for reflection.
- Don't introduce too many new things at once. Aim for one new approach or idea in each service and gradually introduce ideas. The congregation will become used to a varied diet.
- Arrange an interesting programme so that there are not too many jumps and changes of gear!
- All-age worship needs to include elements for everyone, so that it is neither a children's celebration with a little 'word' for the adults or a traditional hymn thrown in to keep adults happy, or an adult service with a song or game suitable for children to enjoy.

Activity

The current emphasis on active learning in the educational world has a great deal to teach us. All-age worship needs to push people a little so they can learn creatively. This is the most effective method for us to learn new skills and information. We are much more likely to remember things that we saw and we felt and we tried out, than things that are just said to us. Therefore, throughout all our worship – the singing, prayer, Bible interaction – we need to be actively encouraging activity!

- *Active songs*. Actions, clapping, raising hands and standing introduce action into our sung worship. An inclusive all-age church accepts that some people will want to be very active and others less so. Generations can learn from each other and demonstrate the importance of involvement, rather than passive observation.

- **Dance and movement**. Not everyone appreciates seeing or taking part in dance in worship, but for others it is a very valuable way of communicating and celebrating the love of God. Dance can be prepared by groups of all ages, male and female and can be accompanied by worship songs or other music. Dance may include the use of flags and streamers. Dance in worship should never become merely a performance but rather something that encourages the watcher to new insights and worship.

- **Giving**. The 'offering' need not be a miserable point in the service when people forget that God really loves a cheerful giver! Make this more active by asking people to bring their gifts to a certain point, pass around a hat (literally!) and play cheerful music.

- **Prayer**. There are many ways to be active in prayer. If prayer is to have any real meaning we need to be as excited about communicating with God as we are making contact with a long-lost friend. That sense of excitement and expectation is for many, best demonstrated through interacting and spontaneity.

- **Fun**. Active games that include movement and reinforce the theme, quizzes which all people can join in with, and movements or responses to a catch-phrase during the story all help to make all-age worship fun. Some adults need permission to relax and have fun, but once they do they should enjoy it and learn through it.

- **Learning**. Teaching is not always best received when coming from one person at the front. All-age worship provides a flexible opportunity to look at the word of God together in smaller groups and discuss what it may be saying. There could be an active introduction to the Bible passage and theme before getting into groups, if the building and furniture allow.

- **Making and doing**. I am often involved with churches holding all-age weekends. They meet as a whole congregation on the Saturday to do creative things on a set theme in mixed age groups, much of which is taken and used as part of the all-age service the following day. The activities could include songs, dance, painting, drama, prayer, poetry, flower-arranging, banner-making, cookery, choral speaking, model-making and so on…the list really is endless! For more ideas see Hands on Bible Creativity (SU) Tracy Woodsford.

Music and Song

For many people music and singing is a key element of worship and a great tool for communication with God. Here is an opportunity to learn doctrine and theology. If we are aiming for multi-sensory worship then music has a major part to play.

- **Music behind words**. Appropriate, non-intrusive background music playing behind prayers, confession or during the talk, can help people focus on what is being said. If you weave a simple song in with responsive prayers there is a cohesion to that part of the service.

- **Music as a gift**. The ability to play a musical instrument is a skill and a gift from God. Church music groups vary greatly in style and

Think about...

Who has a say in the songs used in all-age worship?

How are they chosen, from what range of books and who is consulted in the process?

Is it time to review the list and reintroduce some golden oldies or bring in some fresh songs?

quality, but however great (or otherwise) they sound, they are providing opportunities for people to develop their gifts. All-age worship should ideally be led by a music group of all ages, with experienced and learning adults alongside experienced and learning children and young people.

- *Music to set the atmosphere*. Playing a song or having a music group leading a few songs before the service formally begins, brings people together.

- *Song pitch*. Some new worship songs and many traditional hymns are pitched too high for most congregations. Take care in the choices of songs so that the congregation does not end up sounding like a cats' chorus on a bad day! Musically, a range of just over an octave C to D will be possible for most children. Adults can usually manage a wider range. Teenage boys will struggle with pitch and singing for a whole lot of other reasons!

- *Song traditions*. Most all-age congregations will be looking for a range of songs to use in worship. Despite the yearning many of us have to be up-to-date and cutting-edge, we are still part of a church whose traditions go back over 2,000 years. The first believers, meeting in secret, used spiritual songs and hymns in much the same way as David did hundreds of years before and as we do today. While there is a place for 'said' services, there is also an important role for singing as an integral part of the whole.

• **Mixing it**. Always aim for a balance between songs that are more suited to young people and songs that are preferred by more traditional people. We do not want to alienate whole chunks of the worshipping community because we refuse to sing anything written before the Victorian hymns of the 1800's, or after the 'Seek Ye First' generation of the 1970's! A mix of different styles, choosing a good range and not overdoing songs avoids the worship feeling tired or repetitive.

• **Traditional hymns**. These are meaningful not only to older members of the congregation but may also be reassuring to people who go to church occasionally. Traditional hymns have a lot to teach us through their words. This is confirmed by the recent trend for contemporary worship songwriters to set traditional hymn words to new music. However, the hymns chosen need to be selected carefully, considering the tune, the words, the number of verses and the terms used in the lyrics.

• **Current worship styles**. Proceed with caution! There is a move towards songs which are very strongly led from the front and are therefore performed by the singers or worship leader. An ideal worship song would be one that everyone finds easy to learn and to sing, with clear ideas rather than abstract concepts. It is good to introduce new music, but always consider the ability of your musicians to deliver the song, the simplicity (or otherwise) of the melody and the relevance of the words.

- **Children's worship and praise**. Many children's songs are full of teaching and worship, communicated in a lively way with appropriate words. But some songs patronise children with banal words! As a child I learned much of my theology and many Bible verses through the songs I sang, songs which were modern for their day. We don't want children to have to unlearn something later in life that they thought was true but wasn't!

- **Action songs.** It is a fundamental error to assume that children can only worship if there are actions involved! Action songs have their place and if nothing else adults can join in and call it occupational therapy! But children and young people are capable of worship without actions if they are led well and the songs chosen are understood.

- **Signing and singing**. Many schools now encourage all children, including those who do not have communication difficulties, to learn some basic sign language. This is a very powerful tool in all-age worship, as it is often suited to slower, more worshipful and reflective songs. Sign language gives physical focus for the words and helps people of all ages connect with the meaning. But remember – like everything else, it should be used sparingly and not overdone.

Prayer

Prayer is another key element of worship yet something which continues to be a challenge in many all-age services. Prayer is so much more than intercession, and fresh approaches are desperately needed in our wordy, busy churches.

- **Prayer with all ages**. Prayer, like all of the other components in worship, needs to be active and to involve everyone. There is no place for one adult to stand at the front droning on while children fidget and adults think about plans for the rest of the day.

- ***Prayer by all ages***. It is possible for all ages to lead prayer from the front or to pray in small groups. It is right for young people to speak to God and listen to him. Adults do not have a monopoly on the heavenly channels of communication! Help different families or groups to lead the prayers.

- ***Prayer can be quiet***. In our activity-driven world, many people find it hard to stop and be quiet. Prayer in all-age worship should include times when nothing is said. To help people access quietness, a gentle worship song could be played or encourage focus on a candle, banner, window or cross. This takes away the harsh edge of silence while still allowing God to speak.

- ***Prayer is personal***. In any all-age service there should be time for people as individuals to speak and listen to God. Confessions should be taken slowly and explained rather than just being words to plough through. Younger children may need help with personal prayer activities, or when the congregation is asked to write a few words to God and bring them to the front to be placed on a prayer tree or into a prayer basket.

• **Prayer is corporate**. There is a great sense of unity in having a whole congregation saying the same thing at the same time. Using responsive prayers can help maintain the attention of everyone as well as expressing unity of purpose and a corporate commitment to worship. This is particularly suitable for those who struggle with literacy when a familiar response or phrase is repeated.

• **Prayer can be ministry**. One of the most powerful moments I have experienced when leading all-age worship was to see hundreds of adults kneeling while children and teenagers stood, laid hands on them and prayed for them. This said it all – children and young people can minister to others through praying for them under the guidance and nurture of adults.

• **Prayer can be prepared**. Some people who are asked to lead prayers are very happy to do so as long as they can prepare their prayer beforehand. The expected length, language and content of such prayers should be carefully explained. Prepared prayers could easily be combined with gestures or physical movements to help maintain involvement.

• **Prayer can be visual**. Someone may share a prayer request briefly. A focus point for prayer keeps the congregation on track. Displaying key words and subjects for prayer, projecting images of places or people onto a screen, or using visual aids to communicate the focus of attention helps too. There is no reason to maintain the rather restrictive 'hands together, eyes closed' approach to prayer.

- **Prayer can be physical**. Prayer can involve movement, by turning around, facing different directions, sitting, standing and kneeling. Prayer can be expressive by holding arms up, holding hands out, using thumbs pointing up and down, moving forwards and back.

Think about...

What can be done to freshen up and restore the place of prayer in your all-age worship services?

Is prayer central to worship or tacked on at the end?

Be honest – does it give you a sense of joy or a feeling of despair?

- **Prayer can be an expression of unity** by getting into groups, gently connecting with those around, or forming a chain of prayer along each line.

- **Prayer can be intimate** by lying face down on the floor with a group of others, with heads in the middle, or by forming a rugby scrum. People vary in how comfortable with different prayer activities they feel, but as long as the activity is well-communicated and not done to death, most people will go along with it.

- **Prayer can be extemporary**. While it is right to prepare fully and properly for worship and to be aware of the time, sometimes God might want to take things in a new direction. In the right situation extemporary prayers during a time of quiet can be very helpful.

- **Prayer is answered**. We often fail to recognise or even notice when God has answered prayer. Build in opportunities for children, young people and adults to report back on what God is doing in their lives and how prayer has been answered. This can be done by lighting a match, and the interviewee speaks about answered prayer for the time it takes for the match to burn down! Be aware of safety issues!

• *Prayer should continue*. Encourage people to continue to pray throughout the week, not just when all-age worship takes place. Let people show their commitment to each other by sharing prayer needs.

The Bible

The Bible is important! Our worship should be centred on God's Word, what it has to say to us about the situations when it was written, and what it has to show us about the way we each live our lives at school, church, home, work and in the community. But the use of the Bible in worship can be dry, unimaginative, tedious and something that adults do! The living Word deserves living approaches!

• *Loud and proud*. Some people are scared of doing readings and fear that they will make mistakes and be criticised. The reader should be well prepared and confident as the words are spoken.

• *Relevant words*. There are many translations of the Bible available now, so there is no excuse for an all-age service using readings from a translation with antiquated language. However poetic and beautiful the language might be, you should always be asking the question: 'Does this help people of all ages to understand God's Word?'

Think about it...

What was the last reading of the Bible you heard during an all-age worship service? Give marks out of ten for:

☐ Preparation beforehand
☐ Audibility
☐ Confidence of delivery
☐ Use of different voices
☐ Translation chosen

☐ Introduction of the passage
☐ Liveliness of delivery
☐ Suitability for all ages
☐ Relevance of the passage
☐ Attentiveness of the congregation

Add up the marks. If you're on less than around 80 it suggests that there's work to be done!

• **Different delivery**. Use a variety of voices from various places when the Bible is read.

• **Dramatic delivery**. It can be as simple as dressing the reader in a costume appropriate to the passage, or by using the Dramatic Bible, or if a number of people act out the passage and speak their parts. If the sound system is good this will bring God's Word right into the lives of the listeners.

• **Selective passages**. It is vital to think of the 'consumers'. There are parts of the Bible not suitable for children to hear yet. That isn't to say that we should completely ignore chunks of God's Word, but it is important to select passages that are not going to cause confusion. The more difficult passages can be explored better at the appropriate level in age-group meetings and cell groups. Sticking rigidly to a lectionary reading which contains disturbing images, for example, is inevitably going to cause concern.

- **Promoting the Bible**. How far does your church actively encourage people of all ages to read the Bible throughout the week? Scripture Union provides Bible reading resources for children and young people. Help is needed in how to use such guides. (It is not just young people who need help either!) Parents need support in nurturing their own children's spiritual development. Bibles in pews or readings presented on an acetate or Powerpoint, encourage people of all ages to follow the passage themselves when it is read.

- **Repetition or Reinforcement?** There is a delicate balance between a nice, accessible, narrative Bible reading with a clear story and a passage that supports the teaching. Very often the passage chosen is a story, which is then repeated in a dramatic storytelling afterwards. If the Bible passage is read well it seems pointless to repeat it in another way. If possible, introduce non-narrative readings to support the story and open people up to the breadth of teaching in the Bible.

- **God's visible words**. Technology can really bring God's Word to life. For example, during the reading key words and phrases could be flashed up as they are said, or pictures, images and sound effects can support the text. The whole of the passage can be reproduced to be read in unison or the reader and congregation can take it in turns with alternate verses. For those who know how to put visuals together, this can take minimum preparation but delivers maximum impact. Experiment!

Teaching

One of the familiar criticisms of all-age worship is that the teaching is shallow. We all know that Jesus called on people to have a simple, but not simplistic, faith and to approach God's Word with humility rather than arrogance. Earlier we mentioned the phrase 'keep it short, keep it simple'.

- **Short**. There are very few environments where people now expect to learn by just being talked at for long periods. In our visual age it is far more likely that church members of all ages will remember what they do rather than what is said. A short message can have amazing power and great shock value!

- **Simple**. Those that want in-depth teaching and Bible study can get that during other services and in house groups. One simple, clear message put over in a memorable way is immensely refreshing. Such a message will have a maximum of three clear points and that is not just for the children's benefit but for everyone.

- **Clear**. The complexities of putting together a rounded, thematic all-age service can mean that the theme and teaching message get lost somewhere along the way. Repetition means information is reinforced, not lost. There should be clarity in the teaching which draws on the songs, prayers and activities to bring the teaching to a head. Young people can often see things more clearly than cynical adults, so why shouldn't they do the teaching sometimes?

- **Well-delivered**. The importance of enjoyment in an all-age service includes the teaching part too. The person assigned to do the teaching needs to think how to communicate all that has been learned in a memorable way. Visuals on screen, props or responses always help.

- **Letting it grow**. There is room for being radical and missing out the teaching slot occasionally! If the service has been clearly themed, with elements of discovery, discussion and activity, the 'talk' may be unnecessary.

Resourcing all-age worship

There are many resources to help churches develop worship and teaching to all ages. Scripture Union's Light materials have clear links across the age groups as well as providing activities, prayers and talk outlines for all-age worship. There are many books of prayers and prayer ideas, and numerous songbooks and CDs of more up-to-date adult, youth and children's worship. You can find drama scripts and craft ideas in many resource books. Search in your local Christian bookshop or check out publishers' websites. Make a firm mental note of ideas that will work and use them, soon.

The greatest resource of all, however, is the people! Through interaction, activity and the gradual development of their gifts, everyone in the church should have a valid role to play in delivering all-age worship and encouraging others in it. You may have to invest a great deal of time, energy and creativity to get things moving, and it could take a while! I see signs of hope and glimmers of life – I hope you can too.